T0116351

Grosmutti Gedichte

The Life of a Pioneer Woman
in Northern Wisconsin

Trafford Publishing Ltd.

Patrick Mathias

 www.trafford.com

North America & international
toll-free: 1 888 232 4444 (USA & Canada)
phone: 250 383 6864 ♦ fax: 812 355 4082 ♦ email: info@trafford.com

Contents

Glossary

German	English
Danke schon, nette fraulein.	Thank you, nice lady.
Die Deutsche Frauen	*The German Women*
Gehst du auch in die kirche?	Do you also go to church?
Ja.	Yes.
Welche kirche?	Which church?
Catolische.	Catholic.
Ach! Der Teufel hat dich schon!	Oh! The devil's got you already!

Grossmutti Gedichte / **Grandma Poems**

German	English
Grossvater Was Streng	*Grandfather was strict/strong willed*
Henrietta und die fulle mund	*Henrietta and the full moon*
Matts! Grosse schlange!	Matts (nickname for Mathias)! Big snake!
Mein und nichts.	My way or no way.
Nein	No
Nicht gut	Not good
Nicht mein frau,	Not my wife,
Sie ist in bett.	She is in bed.
So Wie so.	That's the way things go.
Vati	Nickname for father
Was machst du da?	What are you doing there?
Wo gehst du hin?	Where are you going?
Zum Grossvater in Amerika.	To my grandfather's in America.

Dedication

Ever since I was a boy, Gramma Mathias told me stories of her passage from Hamburg to Baltimore, of her struggles as a pioneer in northern Wisconsin, and of the ups and downs of the logging industry in Rib Lake.

During the springs of 1986, '87, and '88, I stayed with Gramma while I cut and peeled popple in Rib Lake. We were alone, and since Gramma was such a wonderful story teller, I had the opportunity to listen and record a few bits of her life.

I'll never forget the picture of Gramma sitting in her armchair in the front room, feet up on the hassock, her homemade thin quilt over her legs. She telling story after story, me scribbling madly, asking questions, then writing some more. We'd do three or four poems an evening, for two or three nights in a row. Then we'd just relax and talk, enjoying each other, knowing the pressure was off.

Whenever I had a Gramma Poem published, I'd make a copy and send it to her. I had to—she was a partner in the writing.

When I'd written the 25th poem of the collection, I decided I'd better start revising.
She wasn't getting any younger and the writing was my responsibility now.

On March 26, 1989, while much of this manuscript was being prepared for publication as a chapbook, Gramma died. She was ninety-three. Though she never saw the completed project, much of what she stood for is still alive: in this book, in the people she touched, in me. This book is dedicated to her; it has to be.

Other people have had experiences like Gramma's, but many take them to the grave. I salute her pioneer spirit, her strength, but most of all her courage to talk about the times that weren't happy. To tell us that life is good, but not a story where things are handed to us like so many roses.

This is a story of Elizabeth Mathias: A German immigrant (born in Josefalva, Austria on January 1, 1896) who never made it past the fifth grade.

It's the story of courage and honesty: it's the story of ourselves. It's simply a story from Gramma to you. We hope you enjoy it.

Patrick Mathias
January 2009

Memories of Passage

They sailed from Hamburg in 1898.
When the sea got rough, Gramma was strong,
"Full of piss and vinegar," she says now.

"I was alone because my mother,
aunt and gramma all got sick--oh
what a time I had! Everyone would ask
'Wo gehst du hin?' I'd answer
'Zum grossvater in Amerika.'"

She still remembers like it was yesterday
not ninety years ago. Like the honey
the Koenigs served on thick, white bread
when they first arrived in Rib Lake.

What a contrast to onions, fried
in pig lard, poured over biscuits
on board the Huntcher.

And watching her grandma and grampa
build their cabin east of town,
both working on a pine stump.
How her gramma found the four-foot bull snake
underneath, screamed "Matts! Grosse schlange!"
and he swung the axe around.

She still remembers the blade,
a double-bit, hitting the snake hard, full,
watching the stroke lop off the big head.

Oh, life was good in America
for little Lizzie: a chatterbox
who'd live to see telephones,
cars, and microwave ovens.

To see her grandsons logging popple,
from land she bought with money
saved, by selling pigs and honey.

Zondlo's Tavern—1898

Matthias and Emma sent money,
"Our kids come too," they told the neighbor.
Seven sailed from Hamburg in 1898,
built next to the big log house.
It was late November.

Winter was cold that year,
Matthias and Emma talked little.
Finally she said, "Four is enough.
We can't feed one more."

Matthias never argued, never said goodbye.
"When you want me back,
you'll have to come and beg."

The food ran out in February,
the gnawing cold made her crawl.

Elizabeth watched all this,
a small girl with good ears.
Saw her aunt grow thin with thirteen kids--
never smiling.

Zondlo's tavern stands there now.
Two pool tables, eight stools, and two gas pumps.
A pine dance floor covers the homestead plot.

I stare out at Highway 102,
wonder what they saw when they looked out.
If their windows were glass,
and doors had hinges.

Whether they'd dance now
if they had a chance.

She Was Four

She was four that August, 1900,
bought their first cow for a dollar.
"Hated kids," she says today.

Even at four she was nosy,
"Inquisitive, so I had to check it out."

Somehow she ended up in the open well,
hanging onto a wooden bucket,
eight feet below ground, splashing
water to stay afloat.

Her father watched it from the back
porch, hauled her up, and beat her
with a stick. Should've known
better than to chase the cow.

That night she cried as she lie
in her strawtick bed, just above
the dirt floor. Careful not to cry too loudly,
or her dad would wake in the room
they all shared,
the log house just six weeks old.

Their first winter in America was coming fast,
but they weren't ready. Not for winter,
cold winds, or the six empty mouths
that needed feeding.

A Dress to Bury Her In

Gramma caught pneumonia when she was six
(doesn't remember how, now),
so her dad carried her two miles
to town. Been in America two years,
hadn't saved enough to buy a horse.

She saw the doctor, then stayed in town
with the Schisslers (aunt and uncle on the lake).
"I can still hear the water lapping
on the shore when the wind blows
just right," she says.

One day Dr. Ignatz came by,
told the Schisslers she'd be dead by noon
the next day. So aunt Bernita
walked uptown, bought some cotton fabric,
made a dress to bury her in.

But the fever broke by morning,
surprised the doctor, the undertaker, too
(I think).

"I got a new dress out of it," she says now,
and smiles a distant smile.

Hard Work, Loneliness, and Bad Water

Tony's first wife died of typhoid,
drank the water before they boiled it.

You see, the old hotel sat on the edge
of Rib Lake. They had no well so they pulled
it up in barrels, used it for cooking and drinking.
Hedwig got careless, died in early 1906.

And left four kids and the hotel for Grampa,
did his best but kids come after customers,
never enough time for both. After six years
he met Lizzy, married a hand, accountant,
one heck of a mother.

Time for a change he promised her,
and dug a well near the kitchen.
Now they could pump clean water,
without the bother of boiling, the worry
of losing another woman.

To this day she remembers walking
past the old hotel (then a nanny
for the Marschkes).
The four kids sitting on the porch,
the smallest cried unceasingly,
unnoticed by the others.

How she stopped and asked him why he cried,
but he couldn't say. Two years old and
something missing, he didn't quite know what.

The oldest had it worst though. Her aunt
took her to Medford, raised her 'til
she turned eighteen. Never did come back.

But every Sunday they visited her.
Lizzy hitched the horse and wagon,
gathered all the kids,
drove the thirty miles to Medford.

"Got to keep a family tight," she said,
and added five boys to the lot.

A Little Girl Watching Corners

Matthias Ehreneich worked hard,
cut pine and pulled it out.
Spent three weeks in the woods,
got two days off and did it again.

After two years he sent for his eldest:
Kris and Magdelena came with families,
brought Alois as well.
Wasn't room so they built a shack nearby.
A good man, Matthias.

Emma said it was "nicht gut" to have more kids.
Held her ground and one day he left,
walked into the woods for good.
Wouldn't return until she begged.

She tried to live.
But three weeks food goes fast in winter,
especially northern Wisconsin, 1890's.
Four kids and nothing growing.

After two months she sent word,
she'd not deny his rights again.
Kids and fists:
nothing more than in any other shack.

"It was all the same," said Gramma,
who watched, then cried when she was alone.
Saw her dad slam Appalonia's head against a tree,
took two hours to wake her up.

Still she listened and smiled at supper,
a lot to eat and plenty of heat.
They all liked it here in America--
though roses don't grow
in the rocky Wisconsin soil.

Henrietta Und Die Fulle Mund

"Gehst du auch in die kirche?"
"Ja."
"Welche kirche?"
"Catolische."
"Ach! Der Teufel hat dich schon!"

Henrietta didn't like her new daughter Lizzy.
"Catholic!" she said,
and lit a fire
when the moon was full.

The sheriff was puzzled,
three fires in two months--
always at full moon.
Put a man on watch from dusk to dawn.

The sentry saw a match flare:
yelled "Was machst du da?" at the bent figure.
The lumber pile caught fire
as he pulled the trigger.

Henrietta died instantly.
The slug went through her spine,
between the shoulder blades, just below the neck.
Put a hole in her husband's coat.

Lizzy prayed for her in mass on Sunday,
asked God to spare her soul.
The sentry asked forgiveness--
didn't mean to shoot an old, deaf woman.

Her husband shook his head,
muttered at the casket:
"Nicht mein Frau,
Sie ist in Bett."

Frozen Linen

Winters were tough in northern Wisconsin,
1917, forty below for three weeks straight.

Lizzie married Grampa, and the Central Hotel,
washed linen every Monday and Thursday.

Used a washboard and rinsing tubs,
carried linens from twenty five rooms outside,
to crackle freeze on steel lines.
Had her older kids carry them in,
draped them over chairs and couches.

In mid-March, 1918,
the chimney sparked, fire erupted.
Everyone got out, but the hotel was hot ash.

Gramma thought of wash and rebuilding.
"Let's put a porch on the new hotel;
one that has an upstairs too."

It was up by April,
with a two-story front porch,
clothesline, and a Roebuck ringer washer.

Lizzie smiled on Mondays and Thursdays,
saw how much better things were now.
Easier to make due while fighting winter,
frozen sheets, and a bed of ashes.

Rib Lake: 1920's

Three weeks in the woods was a long time;
loggers came out with pockets bulging.
Room and board in the woods was paid.

They'd come to Rib Lake,
big mill town with two hotels:
one with a tavern, one without.

The Central Hotel, dry,
filled all twenty-five rooms--
even the "Ram Pasture" on the second floor:
one room with six beds.

Took in half what the National did,
with only fourteen beds.
Served until the roll was gone,
three weeks' pay in one night.

Hard for the Central family,
trying to make it with five kids,
and competition.
Offered clean rooms, fresh venison, a fair price.

Still they made it,
watching Freek walk uptown,
carrying his bankroll.

And the loggers went out to camp,
vowing not to drink again,
collecting three weeks' pay.

While Freek unloaded every third week.
Restocked the shelves with whiskey again,
knowing they'd be back.

The Circle of Pain

Satch Kuppitz had a good thing going.
Every day he'd meet the Chelsea train at 9 a.m.,
rode the Banks's Dray Line down there.

Picked out the new faces, promised
them a free hot meal,
plenty of bourbon.
"A hearty welcome to Rib Lake," he'd say.

After drinks he'd take them for a drive
with his team and wagon, point out
the rocky Wisconsin soil. Green fields
with big white stones: "The sheep come
with the place if you buy it now."

Most of the time they did,
and Satch was at the station
in the morning. Nothing new:
buy land cheap, sell it steep,
use bourbon to dull the senses.

Poor men with families scratched
poor land, plowed between the biggest stones.
But it gets cold in northern Wisconsin,
when you're alone and nothing's growing.

Like the Ellisons out on Little Rib Road,
just enough time to build a shack,
buy a few cows. Determined to make it,
so they kept the cows inside that winter.
Sold milk to buy the hay.

The kids grew up fast out there.
Picked rocks all day, milked cows,
built fences.

Didn't want to leave town quickly,
quietly, like those who didn't make it.
To give the deed back to old man Kuppitz,

who'd sell it again to connect the circle;
start with pain and end with it.

Just Another Wisconsin Logging Town

Rib Lake, early 1920's,
virgin pine in all directions.
Forty-five inches across the stump.

Lumber yard was always full,
trains pulled in three times a day.

Tanning mill had hemlock bark piled forty
feet high, worked leather twenty hours a day.

And two hotels catered to loggers,
came into town every three weeks.
Carried a wad of money,
and an itch for company.

The Central Hotel,
twenty-five rooms and fresh venison
year round. Best food in town.
After cooking fifteen years in the camps,
Henry Mathias knew his business.

National Hotel boasted a tavern;
got a fresh supply of bourbon whiskey
every third week.

And on the Monday of week four,
the owner John Freek walked uptown,
carrying a roll of bloodmoney.

Everyone in town watched,
tight-lipped, as he made his way--
but that was his business.

In a northern Wisconsin logging town,
strong Germans worked to live.
And didn't say a word.

Wisconsin, Logging Camps, and Bad Money

Kris Winkle came into town,
been three weeks at Fawn Valley Camp.
Had a full roll and a new idea.

His friends had been complaining.
Got drunk, drugged some said,
at the National Hotel.
Had their pay lifted.

Decided to play it drunk, pass out,
see if John Freek would take him.

By midnight the National was cooking,
bourbon bottle on every table--
each man screaming to be heard.

Kris Winkle slumped in the corner by the bar.
Freek stooped, dragged him
out of the side door.
Reached into Kris' side pocket,
pulled out folded news print.

And got a knee in the groin,
a broken nose, and three teeth knocked out.

Kris said he'd kill him next time,
even if it happened to a friend.

And Kris Winkle made County Sheriff the next
year, won the election by a landslide.
Wasn't afraid to tackle problems,
tough enough to knock a grown man down.

Still Freek walked uptown every three weeks.
Broad daylight, carrying his bankroll.

Bought the IGA with it,
all the townspeople say.
Passed it on to his family.
Bad money, they say. Bad money.

Die Deutsche Frauen

Vati was shot in '43.
Emma and Alois stopped crying,
found cookies, smiles and a German tongue--
all in Rib Lake, northern Wisconsin.

They'd left Berlin without a dime,
borrowed the thousand marks for travel.
Got a job in town working cheese;
ate cabbage 'til they paid it back.

They came to the Central Hotel one night,
no money, needed a place to stay.
Gramma smiled, said there's always room,
and left preserves outside their sauer door.

In three months Emma married a Greenwood man,
had two thousand acres and a pine tree farm.
Plenty of work so Alois went with them.
Gramma smiled at the horse and wagon.

November 1985, Gramma opened her back
porch door, saw two Germans on the step.
"Only God knows how you carried us," Emma said
slowly. And they took her to Zondlo's for supper.

It's good to see love,
not memory that fades when things get better.
Obligation to an old gray woman?

She kept them alive on cold, dark nights,
put bottles of herself outside their door.
"So wie so," whispers Gramma
as she walks into her empty house.

And I Told Him So

Georgie Huffman courted Gramma,
wanted her to pay for dances.
After all, she was working.

Threw hay and milked
cows for Gerschtburger,
made $1.50 a week.

Dances cost a dollar,
she saw he wasn't worth it.
"Never would amount to much," she thought,
and told him so.

His mother cried,
and a year later Georgie went to Germany.
WWI--everybody went.
Came back with a French wife.

Gramma's eyes sparkle when she tells
how the French woman took in wash.
Made money for bills and food,
while Georgie fished for crappies on Rib Lake.

"He never amounted to anything," she said.
"And I told him so."

Grossvater Was Streng

Grossvater was streng,
strong fist and a straight back.
Always two ways: mein und nichts.

Ran the Central Hotel with a kind heart,
though--always room for one with nothing
but tough luck and a promise.

His nine kids knew no gray zone.
He said it, they did it, or they tasted
the back of his hand. Swing first,
then answer questions, or ask them.

Like the time Hank snuck the truck out,
picked up Brick Johnson, drove out to the beach.
Grampa saw him pull back in the barn,
chased him to the third floor bathroom.

Hank shut the door and locked it,
hung outside the window by his fingertips,
screaming that he'd jump
the minute anyone came in.

Gramma heard it from the kitchen,
knew that Grampa hadn't,
already half deaf you know.
Ran upstairs to stop a death perhaps.

So Grampa waited at the bottom
of the stairs, gave Hank his due in time--
both knew it was coming.

But the family stuck together,
especially when it meant putting meat
on the table, like in the old country.

The oldest didn't have to be told
to steal back deer hides from the warden's
car. To stuff two Holstein calf skins in the sack.
Grampa standing on the porch,
listening to charges, nodding his head.

Told to appear in county court
the next morning, be there at eight o'clock sharp.

The whole family waited.
By ten a.m. the mood was tense,
knew it was good when he came alone.

Later the kids laughed around
the kitchen table; Gramma told the story
when Grampa was out.

How his second cousin laughed,
nervously at first--
when the warden dumped two calf skins
on his desk. Then threw it out of court.

Hard on a judge, or kids
when a family is close and German.
When love is thick, tight and streng.

Old Man Cosky

Old man Cosky liked his bourbon,
"drunk" the men would say
and laugh to his face.

One night Cosky had a tank full,
saw two boys playing under the tramway,
walked up and laid one flat.
Now he laughed out loud,
and one boy carried his brother home.

When Grampa saw it he just walked
uptown, knocked on Cosky's door,
asked him to come outside.
German justice in a 1920 logging town.

He put his fist through the screen
door, "nein" not good enough.
Lost hold of Cosky's neck when the wife
came screaming, waving a butcher knife--
and Grampa said goodbye,
I'll see you again.

He did; between the Kuppitz tavern and
the general store, the way Cosky went home
after bourbon every night.

And Grampa beat him senseless,
with all five young boys watching.
Yelling for them all to get for home.
Except the youngest, who'd been hit
two nights before.

Ten years old and told to hit him hard,
in the middle of his face. To do it again,
not to worry about the blood.
The others stayed too, or ran around the corner,
to peek from the other end, watching justice.

Like Glenn the middle son, who grew
up streng like his father, strived to
stay tough, remembered enough
to tell stories years later.

No tears when he tells the stories,
but the muscles in his jaw tighten
when you speak of Cosky,
his brothers, or German justice.

Untitled (With Reason)

She sees sharply through baggy eyelids,
looks as old as eighty-six.
Listens to boys argue about the cottage.
Money: a corpse for wolves.

Wants to wash her hands,
sees son on son, and wants to spit.
Tearing flesh always makes a bad sound.

Saw a green snake in a dream.
"I could smell it strong," she said.
"So wie so," and shook her head.

Four sons think of wood and block.
What was built so long ago,
takes an hour to tear down.

They meet again to talk,
and tell her they want to be alone.
"Rich get richer," she mutters,
and goes to the kitchen to wash her hands.

Cottage, hunting forties, and the house go up.
Hers and Tony's for so long,
not her business anymore.
She smiles and turns the water on.

Doesn't bother her to hear one say:
"Every dog has his day."
And watches the water swirl downward.

County C Homestead Revisited

We kicked snow from rock and logs,
couldn't find fireplace or rusty pump.
Big Indian rock gone too.

She sat in the truck as we looked around,
dug for pieces of pain and hunger.
Pointed to an old oak:
"That's the tree he used for beatings."

She didn't say "Let a dead dog lie,"
but smiled and told us about the cows.
"We bought three and sold two that year...
one for us to eat."

Dad said Marschke buried it all,
bulldozed a hole and filled it with junk.
Easier than hauling it off his land.
Tears me up to think of pump and hearthstone,
ten feet under corn.

Gramma looked back as we drove away.
Strange I guess,
how smiles tell more than crying.

The Anointed

She sits in a lawn chair
in the late afternoon sun,
near the edge
of the roses she's been clipping.
Wears long, baggy pants and a
bulky winter jacket.

I sit on the grass,
near the roses too,
listening to the story
of the Dietzler woman.

"She got her Last Rites one night,
the story goes (very sick you know),
and immediately stood up and walked
into Rib Lake. Since her soul was saved,
the devil took her body."

"We were Sheephead partners
for thirty years," she says.
"Played three nights a week.
And close to God too."

"And last month, when I was sick,
the priest came to see me.
Anointed my head with oil--
that's only for the very sick you know."

And her eyes look like those
of a child, asking silently
for your opinion.
"Milly Safarski says the devil has the power,
and once you're anointed your body is free."

I tell her it's nonsense, but rumors
and tales stand tall in a small town.
Like the virgin pine her man cut
in the days before chain saws.

"Dumheit" she says.
And with her head cocked
to keep out the setting sun,
she looks hard at me
through silver gramma glasses.

Dancing in Circles

Ernst Zimche escorted Lizzy,
fifteen and danced like the blazes.
He didn't but followed her in circles,
watched her to see what happened.

She walked four miles with him to town.
"I came with you, but if you don't dance
Ernst, it don't mean I'm going home with you."
And she didn't.

Ernst burned.
Kept introducing her to friends
for her to dance with.
Watched them all night long,
but wouldn't learn to dance,
wouldn't take that first step.

In that neck of the woods it was often
that way. Germans watching their girl
dance with someone else. Too proud to stay home,
too stubborn to learn the thing they came for.

A Jew From Milwaukee

Mr. Greenberg came to the hotel
one day in '43. Brought fruit,
hugs for Gramma--
heard her Lawrence died on Okinawa.

"I have a boy fighting too,
don't know where he is, but he's alive.
Don't tell you anything in Special Forces."

A month later the fruit came without smiles.
The Jew's wife had died, heart attack,
only in her forties.

And even Special Forces die in action.
Greenberg's son was one,
died that same year. Baggy eyed,
he walked into Gramma's hotel,
asked for orders, needed hugs.

"I'm all alone now," he told her.
"The business can't go on."

And Gramma looking stern,
says she liked that Jew a lot,
not just a market man,
but a real friend in kind.

The Legend of Lawrence

He was six one, maybe six two,
stood taller than Rib Lake,
at seventeen not afraid of any man.

I know him by his picture,
biggest one on the wall of nine.
Dress blues and picture hazy,
a smile saying I love you.

Three medals hang below,
the Purple Heart in the center.
I look at the brown paneling,
remember Gramma's story.

    I was walking from the cottage
    at Spirit Lake, to the outhouse.
    When I passed the old woodpile
    I heard a voice. It said, "Mother
    Goodbye." Then, "I love you Mother."
    Next day I got a telegram--knew what
    it was before I opened it.

I hear the dishes clinking in the kitchen,
ninety years old, washing plates for grandkids.
Still carrying pictures of the 1800s,
and Lawrence who wasn't afraid
to love his mother, or fight for America.

Next to me on the couch is a pillow:
"Mother O' Mine" from Pendleton, 1942.
My dad's oldest brother hangs on
the wall now. I want to cry too.

Rib Lake Senior Center

The van drops her off at three o'clock;
she walks up the front steps, slowly.

"Been uptown playing Sheephead;
took first place again, won seventy-five cents."

We sit in the kitchen and she unpacks
her bag: a homemade sack over an eight ounce
carton of milk (made it herself,
double thick for insulation). She unties
the drawstring: a sandwich wrapped
in a white napkin; sweet potato in a styrofoam cup.

"They give us too much for dinner,"
she says, and stacks them in the refrigerator,
next to the other cups and sandwiches.

"It's all in how the cards
fall, but the other women say I'm lucky,"
she says. "And a good cook
makes something out of nothing."

At the bottom she finds an old score
sheet. "I got nine twice that day.
Went all the way to seventy."

She crumples it, sets it on top
the wood stove. And with one quick
movement, lifts and moves the cover a crack.
Knocks the paper in with the handle,
and sets the cover back in place.

She smiles and walks out of the kitchen.
And so it is.

Another Small Town Centennial

I page through the history of Rib Lake;
logs, men, and lumber
lined up for the camera.

The stacked lumber covered eighty acres once,
I read out loud.
Gramma says, "Wimpy Wilhelm and that lady
from Greenwood came;
asked all about Tony and the hotel.
Didn't print a word."

The last chance she had
to see her man in pictures,
To have her past published
for all the kids to read.
Things that help old women walk straighter.

I think of the stories:
Grampa shooting deer and partridge
through the crank-out windshield
of the '39 Dodge pickup.

"I haven't read the thing," she says.

I look out Gramma's picture window,
across Railroad Street at the Midfield schoolyard.
And in a flash of Borealis,
through the twinkling of frozen crystal,
see rough cut lumber towering toward the sky.

Central Hotel: Rib Lake, 1984

Across the driveway it still stands,
white, square, three stories tall.
Dad grew up there, only hotel in town.

"I had to crawl under there and rub the pipes;
used hot rags to thaw them out," he said.
I want to crawl in too,
but his past is blocked by mud and cinder.

"The barn stood there,
the chicken coop to the left,
the coal bin was right there."
A lump forms in my throat as Dad points.
All I see is an old one-car garage,
and a sagging clothesline.

He points to the top window:
"That's the one Dad chased
my brother Hank out of."
I want to see too,
but only seven windows appear,
in seven plain apartments.

Let's buy the place, I say.
Build it back the way it was.
But tomorrow he drives to Chicago,
dockwork, and I return to school.

The memories go back too--
money can't buy love.
But it could get that old hotel back again.
For a few seconds I smile.

The building moves as Dad walks away;
makes it hard to focus.
Soon I'll tell my kids:
"Dad said that's where the coal bin was..."

He looks at the pines he planted as a boy,
and I see his eyes are gray.
I put my arms around him--
he seems to know what I can't say.

Together we share the slow walk back.

A Covered Table

An old table in Gramma's shed,
wooden legs, new formica top,
we use it to clean bullheads.

One day I help her clean two chairs.
Bring that table here she says,
people can eat dinner out here.

I carry it;
heavy, solid, 100 years old
she says. Henry's dad made it.

And I'm sorry for the bullhead guts and gills;
they stick, dried, to the top.

And I think of sweat, years, and blood--
how it's worth more than fish,
and rain.

The formica top is wrong.
I want to tear it off,
sand what's underneath,
make it like it was.

I do and Gramma smiles;
it looks good by two old chairs.

To Gramma Lizzy (A Love Story)

I got your card today, early as always.
Not just a card, but love
in a letter. You didn't have to.
A check for bread, eggs, and popcorn.

I opened it in Technical Writing class.
Among graphs and charts you stood
like a log cabin above waving grass;
a picture on County C, just north of 102.

That shack is gone now; rocks
still mark the place--an old rusty pump.
Gramma grew up there,
had Indians in her back yard.

I think of the things you did.
A little girl in coarse clothing,
collecting pennies on the Huntcher.
Smiling "Danke Schon, Nette Fraulein."

Your face, etched in worn field stone,
comes into focus.
I think of chances passed;
love wells, impulse follows synapse.

More than rhubarb pie, "Eat all you want."
Northern Wisconsin at three years old,
barefoot, sleeping on dirt with cornhusks.

Your mom said you never cried,
big eyes always smiling--
"I like it here in America."

A Problem With Health

She woke up at 3 a.m. with a belly ache,
the kind that makes you sick
because you know it's for real.
By 4 a.m. she was on her way to Medford,
lights flashing all the way.

Days of testing showed nothing
but a tumor in her left kidney.
"The only way we'll know it's cancer
is to take it out," they told her.
"At your age it isn't worth it."

And two weeks later she tells
my brother she's loaded with cancer.
"Ninety-two and soon to die," she says.
Bad news travels fast.

Later we find out the x-rays
showed nothing but an old woman;
twisted a bit, gnarled, but in good condition.

I wonder what it's like to be old enough
for sympathy, but too healthy to get it.
Used to throwing hay for sixteen hours
a day, raising nine kids when boys were men
at thirteen, and women married after the eighth grade.

I tell her she looks good
and we hug hard.
It's good to be healthy,
but see she's disappointed.

At the Card Table

She's ninety.
We sit again at the card table for Smear,
Gramma, Glennie and I.
I wonder how sharp she is.

I bid four
(we're playing seven point),
and lead with the ace, follow with the king,
got three points and the boss is my queen.
For kicks, I throw fail and Glennie takes it.
He leads and she tops it with a jack,
and I throw on my joker by mistake.

"Leave it as you played it," she says
and puts her hand out, scoops up the trick.
My face turns red, and I answer my own question,
see her like she is, like she used to be.

A shrewd woman, I've heard them say
uptown, always wins at Sheephead.

They're probably right.
I smile as I realize she set me,
ask her if she wants to play again.

She nods but says she's not sure
what suit to bid in.

Gramma's House

And so, for the third time
in three years, I lie
in the back bedroom. My body
aching from cutting and peeling popple;
feels good to put in seven hours
by noon.

In the house everyone else
is napping. I look up at the portrait
above the bed: Henry and Henrietta Mathias
(her in-laws). At the white ceiling:
cloth covers age cracks.

And remember the days we'd come
to visit, one of us would always get to stay,
get to spend a month with her.

She'd take down her plastic purse
filled with tackle, walk us down to Powers'
pier on Rib Lake. Show us how to catch
perch and bullheads, cleaned them for us
'til we learned how.

Always had time for us, me--even now
we talk for hours. About the old days,
the hotel, Tony (her husband), the colors
of Rib Lake, the Holy Spirit.

I roll over and notice the mattress sags
more now, there are cobwebs above the south
window, but she's still sharp at ninety-two.
"Know when to keep my big mouth shut," she says.

I realize now why I can't sleep:
tomorrow I leave and she'll be gone soon.
It felt good to leave the woods today
(for the last time this season),
but better to know we talked yesterday.
Gramma telling old stories, me making
poems of them, putting her on paper.

She's asleep now, with her teeth
in a cup on the nightstand.
Tomorrow she'll be up at five,
to make coffee and toast,
and to say goodbye with breakfast.

Voices in the Woods
or
The Day Before Tanttar

With chain saw screaming I hear voices.
I look at Glenn, why'd he scream "Hey Pat"?
but he's bent over a tree, ripping bark
with spud in hand.

Again I hear, "Hey Pat--time for a break?"
and look around--nothing but bark flying.

At lunch I ask him if he ever
hears things in the woods.
"Yeah," he says. "I keep hearing you say
that trees are falling. Once I heard you yell,
looked over and the water jug was gone."
There are voices in the woods.

I score a limbed tree, and with the
saw topped out I hear it again:
"Let's go home." I look at Glenn,
stripping bark from a downed tree.
He looks up, smiling, says let's make
this one the last.

Tanttar

A piece of yellow paper,
two by six inches, sits on my front seat:
Tanttar waits for me
to come out of the woods.

Does it mean trumpet blasts?
Or that a man, possibly another logger,
doesn't want me cutting pulp
on my own land?

The abandoned farmhouse
stands across the hayfield.
From it you could've seen my
door open; perhaps a man dressed in plaid,
a big belly and chain saw hands,
smiled as he dropped the paper.

Thought he'd scare us, or make us look
over our shoulders while working popple.
Start to hear voices in the woods.

I think of screaming chain saws,
little brother Glennie and his water jug moving.
"I thought I had it right on this stump."

Only a slip of paper, I say to myself,
doesn't mean a thing. I fold it carefully
and put it in my wallet.

Wisconsin's Other Butter

There's butter in Wisconsin.
Drop a tree and score it,
stick a spud in and pop--
fresh butter.

Sticky sweet and slippery,
the bark falls off in long thin strips.
Twenty-five cents a stick,
worth every penny.

A day later the butter turns pink,
you have to step over peeled sticks
to get fresh ones. Sap and sweat
mingle rotten in gloves and pants,
the butter sweeter, tougher.

And flies like butter,
swarm to the discarded bark
(and pants when you rest).
Twelve hour days are long
but the flies make breaks short,
better to just keep moving.

And yet by five-thirty both sweatshirts
are always wet. I wonder
if butter is inside too, or if
sweat works from the outside in.

Sixty-Five and Still Cutting

Sixty-five and still cutting,
back bent and arms dragging,
belly basketball.

Wimpy works full days though,
knocking trees down and limbing.
Still bunching too--
one of the last of Rib Lake's loggers.

He teaches us, little Glenn and me,
about bark, sap, and skidding.
A quiet man always talking:
"Never had a son to teach,"
he said, and pulls the cord on his Husqvarna.

Wimpy brings the tongs and picaroon.
A fat elbow, too—
said he was done for the year,
going to Vegas for vacation.

It doesn't seem right though,
a place like that for Wimpy:
legs boughed from heavy work,
and bad ankles standing next to slot machines.

From Buttercream to Rose

In mid-June it takes two days
for peeled popple to turn--
goes from buttercream to rose.
Funny how color makes things different.

Up close I see the red in streaks,
like brushed paint. The fallen
bark already rotting;
a three-day old banana peel.

I ask the old woodcutter,
"Who did this?" but Wimpy didn't know.

Funny. You can work with someone
your whole life, never
know his name.

Red comes from inside,
air sucks it out--inevitable for popple,
but still so painful.

You see, once the color's gone it's dead.

A Sketch of Popple

Fifty feet of smooth stick,
no limbs, sap oozing,
slugs sucking life, and flies,
lots of flies.

Bark--pieces eight feet long,
beginning to rot.

Five minutes after the bark's off
it's the slipperiest.
Sap moves from inside out.

Popple is like butter inside,
and people--wrinkled skin on elbows,
like knots under thin bark.
I've seen them.

I scrape bark off with spud
in gentle waves, like the skin
on Gramma's elbows,
smooth, wet, rippling.

The Phone Call

It came last night,
it had to. Silence on the other end.
Between sobs Dad tells me
his mom is dying.

Had a stroke on Tuesday,
left eye droops,
cheeks sag, chin twisted.
I listen to a man I've never
known before, crying on the phone--
something a strong German never does.

"Since Wednesday, she's slipped
a little every day," he said.
"Just a matter of time
before the heart goes. We hope
it fails soon; she's holding
her head pretty heavy now.

Doc Hesse asked about life support
and Dad said no, let her go easy.

At ninety-three that's how she'd want it.
A fighter going down? A pioneer
slipping under?

So this evening, my brother and I
drive down to see her, to say goodbye
before she's gone. To tell her all the things
grandmas live on, die on.

Knowing I'll make the trip again,
soon, with Julie and Zach, to watch
her put beneath the rocky earth
she toiled over, broke by hand with oxen.

But that's another trip you know,
made another day. The toughest thing
is waiting, knowing it too will come.

The Smell of Death

I never smelled it before,
but here with Gramma dying
I know it, like an old friend
at a high school reunion.

In her room it smells sweet, though,
strangely like her home.
And peaceful, the sound of bubbles
as oxygen travels through water.

And Paul sits with her talking of Smear
games past, of fishing bullheads with her
at Power's pier on Rib Lake.
Of cooking things, strange things we'd bring home:
rabbit, squirrel, chipmunk, frog legs,
even a porcupine once.

But this is goodbye, Gramma,
our acknowledgement that
something unpleasant is going to happen.
You know it; I do too.
We can see it in your eyes,
though one sags now,
and the other is hidden behind the hand
you hold to your face.

Though we can't talk,
we watch your left hand move.
I hold your right, wrinkled, smooth
with elastic thin skin.
I see your long finger nails--
especially your right index finger.
A garden not watched closely, you always said...

I watch your lips closely too,
and the corner of your mouth moves.
The side that is motionless
because of stroke moves.

We know you can hear us, know we
came to say goodbye forever.
We can't be sure, but as long
as eyes can see and hearts feel love,
our goodbye will live.
And you Gramma, in it and us,
will too.

An Easter Gift

You did it again,
dying like that on Easter.

You always lived with flair,
style, danced a jig with
your grandkid on your ninety-third.

Born on New Year's Day,
and died on Easter--
even in death you make me smile.

After Dad's phone call
I stayed up--I had to--
you left me with lots to think about.
The manuscript, connecting with you,
and death.

And how we prayed for a quick death,
Paul and I, after coming to see you,
after coming to say goodbye.

Three strokes after the broken hip.
You fell walking uptown for your own groceries,
middle of January, northern Wisconsin.

Paul and I sat by you,
stroking your soft thin skin,
and said goodbye, hoping
you wouldn't linger that way.

So now I lie on the couch
with my family sound asleep,
alone with you again, thinking
of all the gifts you gave:
the gold pocket watch on my tenth birthday,
three silver certificates, and the silver coins--
blackened by the fire that destroyed the old hotel.

An open door and a cookie jar,
the bullhead pliers and fried fish,
spilt flour and apple strudel,
always a warm hug and a place to sleep.

And finally your last gift,
telling us that people do live on.

Say it and be done with it

you'd say. Don't spend all day
flapping your gums, especially when
there's work to do.

Do it honestly, with a big
long hug, drinking in each other's smell,
and say "good-bye."
Do something useful
for someone who needs it.

Keep the poem short you'd say.
A good idea, just keep it short--
others will read it then,
and still have time
to go about their business.

Since this is for them, I will
(knowing you're ready to die,
knowing I could never be).

But I still hang on,
clutching the gramma of fishing
and apple strudel, inventing
conversations we would have had
tomorrow.

Speech During the Rib Lake Centennial, 1981

I am an early pioneer--came to Rib Lake in 1898 and lived here the greatest part of my life.

My late husband "Tony" Mathias and I operated the Central Hotel for fifty-one years. Now I live in an old eight-room house almost as old as I am--eighty years. I was eighty-five years old on January 1, 1981. I am still able to keep up this home, make a big garden, cut a large lawn, and raise lots of beautiful flowers. I like to go for walks too.

I'd like to say one line about Rib Lake, if I may:

    I came from the East, Europe;
    I've traveled out west to Hawaii;
    I've gone up north into Canada;
    Been to the Virgin Islands.

But 100 year-old Rib Lake--that, my dear friends, is my land.

Written By Elizabeth Ehrenreich Mathias at 1 a.m., July 9, 1981.
Introduced by our honorable mayor, John Eckoff.

Obituary

Elizabeth Ehrenreich Mathias, 93, of Rib Lake, Wisconsin died on Easter Sunday, April 27, 1989 in the Rib Lake Health Care Center. She was born on January 1, 1896 in Josefalva, Austria, and two years later immigrated to the United States.

She and her family left Hamburg, Germany in October 1898, and arrived in Baltimore, MD. three weeks later. She made it to Rib Lake by winter and lived in the family homestead on the corner of County C and 102, where Zondlo's Ballroom now stands.

She and her husband Henry (Tony) Mathias owned and operated the Central Hotel in Rib Lake for 51 years, from 1906 to 1957. She was a member of St. John's Catholic Church, The Christian Mothers Association, The Royal Neighbors, The Lehman-Clendenning American Legion Auxillary (for over fifty years), and The Rib Lake Senior Citizens.

Lizzy is survived by four sons (Dan of Green Bay, WI; Hank of Burnsville, MN; Glenn of Palos Park, IL; and Bill of Madison, WI), two stepsons (Walter of Wauwatosa, WI; Raymond of San Clemente, CA), and two stepdaughters (Hattie Taylor of Rib Lake, WI; Bernita Edens of Tomahawk, WI).

She is also survived by four sisters: Mary Banks, Rose Lund, Evelyn Randle, and Barbara DeVine; and by twenty grandchildren, and fifteen great-grandchildren.

Lizzy was preceded in death by her husband Tony in January 1962, and her son Lawrence in July 1944.

Lizzy was one of the pioneers of Rib Lake and dearly loved this area, spending both summer and winter there every year since 1898. She loved to fish and hike, to play Sheephead and Smear, to garden and to bake, and especially loved spending time with her family. Her home was open to family twenty-four hours a day, 365 days a year.

Funeral services were held at 10:30 a.m., on April 29, 1989 at St. John's Catholic Church. She was waked at Dallman Funeral Home from 3:30 -8:30 p.m., on April 28, 1989.

Gramma's Soap Recipe

Ingredients:

    6 lbs beef fat
    2 1/2 pints rain water (cold)
    1 can lye
    2 TBS borax powder
    1/2 C tap water
    1/2 C ammonia
    1 tsp perfume (optional)

Dissolve lye in 2 1/2 pints cold rainwater, in a large glass jar or crock. As the lye dissolves, the mixture becomes hot. Let it cool at room temperature. Melt the fat and strain it into a crock. When cool, add the lye mixture and stir until all the lye has combined with the fat. The mixture should be like thick honey.

Add the borax mixed with 1/2 C water. Add 1/2 C ammonia and 1 tsp perfume (if desired). Mix well and pour into a cloth-lined wooden box. Cut when it is ready to set (about 30 minutes). If you wait too long, it will be too hard to cut.

The soap keeps forever and is an excellent spot remover. It is also very effective on poison ivy. It has also been used as laundry detergent, especially when dried and grated into small particles (the food processor works well).

Biography

Patrick Mathias is the author of *Hunting With Amazing Grace, Notes From the Northwoods, God Shapes Playdough and Other Simple Things,* and *Window Games: Life Changes With Zachary*

He was born in Tomahawk, Wisconsin, then moved with his family to Palos Park, Illinois at the age of two. As a young boy, Patrick spent his summers in the Rib Lake area at the family lake cottage. All four of his grandparents were pioneers in the Rib Lake area.

For the past twenty years, Mathias has taught writing at Itasca Community College in Grand Rapids, Minnesota where he also serves as the faculty advisor for Campus Crusade for Christ. Mathias also works as a free lance technical writer, customized trainer, and as a personal writing coach. He and his wife Julie (his best friend) live in the Grand Rapids area with their three children. They enjoy camping, hunting, fishing and canoeing.

Printed in the United States
By Bookmasters